FLIPPIN' AWESOME!

WATER BOTTLE FLIP
GAMES, TRICKS, & STUNTS FOR EVERYONE!

SARAH DOUGHTY

FOR YOUNG READERS

Racehorse for Young Readers books may be purchased in bulk at special discounts for sales promotion, corporate gifts, fund-raising, or educational purposes. Special editions can also be created to specifications. For details, contact the Special Sales Department, Skyhorse Publishing, 307 West 36th Street, 11th Floor, New York, NY 10018 or info@skyhorsepublishing.com.

Racehorse for Young Readers™ is a pending trademark of Skyhorse Publishing, Inc.®, a
Delaware corporation.

Visit our website at www.skyhorsepublishing.com.

10 9 8 7 6 5 4 3 2

Cover art used under license from Shutterstock.com

Book design by Katie Jennings Campbell

Print ISBN: 978-1-63158-169-4

Printed in China

CONTENTS

HOW IT ALL STARTED

IT WAS THE FLIP HEARD 'ROUND THE WORLD.

The origin of water bottle flipping can be traced back to one gutsy high school senior named Mike Senatore, who strutted onto the stage of his school talent show with nothing but a water bottle and a simple goal: to successfully flip it and land it. With one artful flick of the wrist, he claimed his role as champion of a new and exciting pastime. YouTube posts of Mike's bottle flip earned him instant fame and helped fuel a craze that spread from that North Carolina high school gym to lunchrooms, baseball dugouts, backyards, and playgrounds all over the world.

What does it take to be a part of this flippin' awesome new trend? That's the best part; you don't need fancy or expensive equipment. All you need is time to hone your skills, a steady supply of plastic bottles, and a little old-fashioned determination. Flipping can be done solo or in groups by anyone, anytime, anywhere.

A LOT OF LEGENDS, A LOT OF PEOPLE, HAVE COME BEFORE ME. BUT THIS IS MY TIME.
—USAIN BOLT

When you've figured out how to stick the landing most of the time and you're ready to step up your game, challenge yourself with modified flips, masterful maneuvers, and competitive flipper-versus-flipper target games. Use the enclosed score cards to rack up your points and track all of your wins.

Ready to make your mark in the world of bottle flipping? Grab the closest water bottle, crank the volume on your motivational music playlist, get in the zone, and start nailing those landings. When you think you have reached your peak as a bottle flipper, when you don't think you have enough strength to flip one more bottle or master one more trick, remember: champion bottle flippers aren't born. They're made. Best of luck on your road to victory.

FIND SOMETHING TO FLIP

THERE'S A WHOLE WORLD OF BOTTLES OUT THERE just waiting to be flipped. They come in all shapes and sizes, and while some are easier to manipulate than others, each one has its own set of advantages and challenges.

It may take a little time for you to find the size and style you prefer (and your choices may be restricted to what's easily available in your fridge or cabinets), but eventually all flippers find a bottle that works best for them. Some veteran flippers swear by hourglass-shaped water bottles filled one quarter to one third of the way with water, while others will only work with sturdy, two-thirds-full, flat-bottomed bottles that can sustain hundreds of trials. As you perfect your flip, you'll begin to view just about any bottle in sight as a projectile to be tossed at will. If it's plastic and holds liquid, it has the qualities to showcase your skills and impress everyone around you.

Begin your training with a regular water bottle, but take your game to a whole new level when you're brave enough to try the following variations:

▶ 2-liter soda bottle
▶ Shampoo bottle
▶ Baby bottle (just don't grab it out of a baby's hands)
▶ Milk jug
▶ Reusable sports bottle
▶ 5-gallon water dispenser refill bottle

When choosing your bottle, you may also want to consider the cap size. If you plan to do stunts like the legendary "cap flip," in which the bottle lands squarely on its cap at the end of your trick, you'll have more success with bottles with oversized caps.

HOW TO EXECUTE THE PERFECT FLIP

WITH A BOTTLE IN HAND (filled about one-third of the way with water) and your instincts to guide you, it's time to get in the game. Grab the bottle by the neck just under the cap and swing it gently at your side to gauge the weight and the force you'll need to use. With a flick of the wrist, release the bottle so that it performs a full 360-degree rotation in the air. If you execute the basic flip just right, the bottle will land firmly on its base. If it doesn't land correctly, you'll need to adjust the speed of your toss, the timing of your release, or the amount of water in the bottle. Practice makes perfect with this maneuver, so expect a lot of failed attempts before you develop killer skills and, eventually, total mastery!

THE PLAY-BY-PLAY

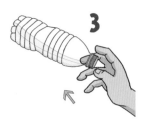

Step 1: Fill the water bottle about a third of the way full.

Step 2: Hold the bottle just below the cap.

Step 3: With a little bit of force, flick your wrist and send the bottom of the bottle sailing up and away from you.

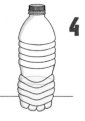

Step 4: If the bottle doesn't land upright, adjust your technique and try again.

Make sure your force and your flick are working together in perfect harmony. Too much of both and you'll get too much flip and less control over the destination; too little of both and you'll toss it to the floor without a circular rotation.

VARIATIONS ON THE BASIC FLIP

BEFORE YOU GRADUATE TO NINJA MOVES, spend some time learning the art of the release. If you want to flip the bottle, you've got to *be* the bottle! These modifications will give you the ninja skills you need to dominate the games and stunts that lie ahead.

I FEAR NOT THE MAN WHO HAS PRACTICED 10,000 KICKS ONCE, BUT I FEAR THE MAN WHO HAS PRACTICED ONE KICK 10,000 TIMES.
—BRUCE LEE

Double Flip: Flip the bottle high enough that it can make two full rotations before landing on its base.

Blind Flip: You guessed this one, right? Just close your eyes and flip.

Twin Flip: Hold a bottle in each hand and flip them simultaneously.

Sailor Flip: Flip a bottle so that it lands on a higher surface.

Behind-the-Back Flip: Flip the water bottle from behind your back and have it land on a surface in front of you.

Between-the-Legs Flip: Similar to the Behind-the-Back Flip, but with this one you toss the water bottle from between your legs.

EMPTY YOUR MIND, BE FORMLESS. SHAPELESS, LIKE WATER. IF YOU PUT WATER INTO A CUP, IT BECOMES THE CUP. YOU PUT WATER INTO A BOTTLE AND IT BECOMES THE BOTTLE.
—BRUCE LEE

THE PHYSICS OF THE FLIP

BOTTLE FLIPPING MAY LOOK SIMPLE, but it is also guided by some pretty cool and sophisticated scientific principles. If anyone hassles you about making a flippin' scene in class or at home with your bottle tricks, just break out the science jargon and call it a physics lesson, because after all, *it's educational!*

How does the water stay in the bottom of the bottle, even when the bottle is upside-down?

The answer is *centrifugal force*. Ever wonder how you stay in a roller coaster when it goes upside-down? Sure, you have seatbelts, but seatbelts aren't the only thing holding you in. Whether or not you can loop around on a roller coaster without falling out is based on the distribution of mass of the people in the roller coaster, how quickly the roller coaster is traveling, and where the coaster's center of gravity lies. You can thank your seatbelt *and* centrifugal force for preventing your untimely death.

Need another analogy? Think about a pail of water. If you hold a pail of water by the handle and swing it around in a fast circle, the water stays put. If you swing it up and stop abruptly or swing too slowly, the water will pour out.

The same goes for the water bottle flip. Your throw is the force, and the mass of the water in the bottle is affected by the gravitational pull. When you have a water bottle that is about one-third full, the centrifugal force during the flip keeps the water at the bottom of the bottle and maintains it as the bottle's center of gravity. The center of gravity is the heaviest part of the bottle.

Proudly recite the following words the next time someone tells you that bottle flipping is a brainless activity: *centrifugal force, axis, torque, angular acceleration.* Then drop the mic.

The rotation of the bottle as it is flipping is made possible by the *moment of inertia*, and how the center of gravity plays off the *axis* of the rotation. This is all affected by how forcefully you flip it (the *torque*) and its positioning as it's flipped (*angular acceleration*).

Why doesn't it work when I flip a full bottle?

If the bottle is completely full, then the weight of the bottle is more evenly distributed. This means that any side of the bottle is fair game for a landing, which results in a bottle rolling away from you and the feeling of utter defeat. If the bottle is about one-third full, the center of gravity stays at the base of the bottle, which means that the base is pulled to the ground first. This makes it the most likely location to stick the perfect landing, crowning you as a genius and a hero.

IT'S NOT THAT I'M SO SMART, IT'S JUST THAT I STAY WITH PROBLEMS LONGER. —ALBERT EINSTEIN

With practice, this becomes less like a physics lesson and more like the stuff of legends. With a casual flick of the wrist and the right amount of water, you'll be sticking sick landings hundreds of yards away after a backflip off a trampoline.

BOTTLE BLING

EVERY GAME HAS ITS PURISTS, and bottle flipping is no exception. Traditional flippers want their skills to take center stage, so they cling tightly to a simple but unremarkable recipe of: everyday water bottle + water. Then there are the true showmen and showwomen who like to add a splash of style to their game. There's room for both of these players in the world of bottle flipping. If you want to add swagger to your bottle and earn points for presentation, try the following substitutions and add-ons:

Bottle Swag Options:

- Duct tape the sides of the bottle, leaving the bottom exposed.
- Roll on glue, then glitter.
- Bejewel the sides with stick-on gems.
- Draw an intimidating face on it, using permanent marker.
- Add a stick-on moustache.

Water Upgrades:

- Add 5–6 drops of food coloring
- Add a handful of glitter
- Add 1 miniature bouncy ball
- Add a tablespoon or more of oil

> I WOKE UP THIS MORNING AND REALIZED: I DON'T HAVE WHAT IT TAKES TO BE AVERAGE.
> —UNKNOWN

MAKE A VICTORY MOMENT SOUNDTRACK

Consider adding these winning tracks
to your highlight reel:

"Centuries" (FALL OUT BOY)
"Try" (PINK)
"Good Feeling" (FLO RIDA)
"Eye of the Tiger" (SURVIVOR)
"The Distance" (CAKE)

TRICK SHOTS

IT'S TIME TO PICK UP A FEW CREATIVE MOVES to show off your incredible flippin' talent. Adjust your water level, your release, and your distance until you've got each of these tricks on lock. Then perform them like a worldwide celebrity.

Capping: Flip a bottle so that it lands squarely on its cap.

TIP: *When "capping," some people start with the bottle upside-down in their hand.*

Action Sequence: Flip a bottle so that it sticks its landing on a skateboard rolling past you.

Skinny Shelf: Flip a bottle into the air so that it does a full rotation and lands on a narrow shelf or railing overhead.

Stairmaster: Stand at the bottom of a set of stairs and flip the bottle so that it lands on a step.

Footie: Flip a bottle off the top of your foot.

Stick Flip: Flip a bottle off the flat end of a hockey stick.

BOOM!!!

CHAMPIONS KEEP PLAYING UNTIL THEY GET IT RIGHT.
—BILLIE JEAN KING

ADVANCED MANEUVERS

THESE EXPERT TRICKS ARE NOT RECOMMENDED for rookies, but they are designed to make the crowd roar. Each one requires a superhuman amount of focus and determination, not to mention loads of free time. Stick to it, though, and you could eventually master these killer moves and earn celebrity status in the world of bottle flipping.

The Catapult

Send a water bottle soaring through the air by placing it on one end of a skateboard and then stomping on the other end. The bottle should land upright or—if you're a true master—on a ledge some distance away. Kapow.

The Swish

Flip a bottle through a basketball hoop so that it lands upright on a table below the hoop or on the ground. Shazam.

For a masterful twist on The Swish, try to shelve or cap the bottle on the back of the basketball rim.

The Hole-in-One

Use a golf club to putt a standing water bottle into the air and land it in a wide container or hole in the ground. Boom.

The B-ball Bounce

Balance a bottle on top of a basketball and hold the basketball out in front of you at waist level. Drop the ball so that the bottle bounces up onto a table. Kabam.

The Hat Trick

Flip a bottle so that it lands on the flattened rim of the baseball cap you are wearing. Cha-ching.

CHAMPIONS AREN'T MADE IN GYMS. CHAMPIONS ARE MADE FROM SOMETHING THEY HAVE DEEP INSIDE THEM—A DESIRE, A DREAM, A VISION.
—MUHAMMAD ALI

The Stacker

Flip a bottle into a corner of a room or desk and then flip a second bottle so that it lands stacked on top of the first. Mind blown.

FLIPPIN' HEROES

YOU WON'T BELIEVE WHAT BOTTLE FLIPPERS WORLDWIDE have pulled off in terms of amazing stunts. Online videos reveal thousands of legendary bottle-flipping moments to inspire your wildest dreams. Here is a sampling of some of the boldest and most creative moves on the interweb:

A Little League player flips a bottle onto a corkscrew playground slide and watches in awe as it careens gracefully off the end of the slide and lands upright in the dirt.

A kid balances a water bottle on the back of his scooter, speeds up a ramp, executes a perfect backflip, and manages to fling the water bottle into the air behind him and land it squarely on the ramp.

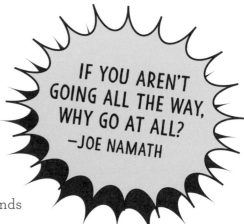

IF YOU AREN'T GOING ALL THE WAY, WHY GO AT ALL?
—JOE NAMATH

Two young girls release their bottles simultaneously and their faces register utter shock as the first bottle lands on its side and the second lands balanced on top of the first!

A boy approaches a soccer ball with a water bottle perched on top of it. He kicks the ball and the bottle flips up and lands upright while the ball soars off toward the goal.

A man flings a water bottle up into the air toward an unlikely target: a towering street lamp. The bottle flips and lands on top of the lamp's curved surface.

A teenage girl flips a water bottle out of her hand and lands it expertly on the top of her sneaker. She casually flips it off her sneaker and watches it land upright on the ground.

A guy stands next to a towering fast food sign. He flips a water bottle high into the air and watches as it sticks a landing beside the golden arches.

GET CREATIVE

Here are some suggestions for pushing the boundaries and adding a fun twist to your bottle-flipping adventures. Be a trendsetter and come up with your own unique ways to play!

- Create an obstacle course with flipping stations. Incorporate bikes, scooters, and sporting equipment of all kinds to make it daring.

- Truth or dare. Sit in a circle and take turns flipping. If your flip doesn't stick the landing, you have to choose truth or dare and sweat it out until you complete the challenge suggested by the person to your left.

- Timed trials. See how many bottle flips you can land in a set amount of time. Flip to the back of the book to record your progress.

- Make a video. Record yourself and/or your friends performing advanced maneuvers and cool tricks.

- Play F-L-I-P, the bottle flipping version of H-O-R-S-E: One player flips and lands a bottle from any distance using any technique. The next player must pull off the same flip to avoid getting the letter F. Be the first to spell out F-L-I-P and you lose the game!

TIPS FOR FILMING YOUR FLIPPIN' VIDEO

When you're flippin' awesome, you'll probably want to share your skills for all the world to see. Here are some tips for creating some killer video footage of your most triumphant bottle-flipping moments.

1. Use a smartphone or a durable action camera mounted firmly on a tripod. Stabilizing your camera prevents shaky footage and puts your moves in clear focus.

2. Film in good light so that your audience can see every detail of your victorious flip stunt.

3. Keep recording. You can always edit out boring stuff later.

4. Do a test run. That way you can make sure that the sound and lighting are just right.

5. Use video editing software to combine shorter clips for a highlight reel or to add a soul-stirring soundtrack to underscore how flippin' awesome you are.

6. Check with your folks first, but consider posting your video online and wait to see if you earn worldwide acclaim.

THE LUCKY 7 BOTTLE FLIP

Lose the cue and skip the pool hall with the Lucky 7 Bottle Flip. By calling your pockets and landing with precision, you'll be sinking the competition in no time. Keep your eye fixed on the 7, but watch out for the notorious 8 ball; it could crush your pool hall dreams. Make each flip a lucky one.

MULTIPLAYER MODE

1. Place the target on a sturdy table or floor.

2. Decide how far away a player should stand from the target and mark this distance with an object or a piece of tape.

3. Choose one player from each team to start.

4. The first player calls out the number of a ball and attempts to "pocket" the pool ball by flipping a bottle and landing it upright on the chosen target. It must land upright with more than half of the bottle's base touching the ball in order to earn points. Some balls carry bonus points (like the 7), while others are risky: a called pocket on the 8 ball wins the game, but pocket the 8 without calling it and your team loses.

5. The turns alternate between teams, with each player getting one flip per turn. The first team to earn 50 points wins.

◎ SCORING

▶ **20 points when you call and pocket the 7 ball**

▶ **10 points for landing a bottle on the targeted ball (a "called pocket")**

▶ **5 points for landing a bottle on a ball other than the one you called (a "pocket")**

▶ **0 points for landing a bottle anywhere else (a "scratch")**

▶ **-10 points when you pocket the 13 ball without calling it**

TRICK SHOT BONUS: If the shooter throws the bottle from behind his or her back and it lands on a ball, the player earns 20 points. If the bottle lands on a ball that was "called," the player's team automatically wins the game.

SINGLE-PLAYER MODE

Try to pocket each ball, leaving the 8 ball last in order to win.

FLIPPIN' FLASH

Test your speed and skill with Flippin' Flash. With just a minute to outplay your opponents each round, only a true master can handle the pressure of this bottle game. Beware of the skull, because it'll bury your chances of glory with one unlucky miss. Only a cool and calm bottle baron will swiftly flip enough to win it all in this high-intensity game.

Extra item needed:
cell phone or kitchen timer

MULTIPLAYER MODE

1. Place the target on a sturdy table or floor.

2. Decide how far away a player should stand from the target and mark this distance with an object or a piece of tape. Arrange 6–12 water bottles in a line next to the marker.

3. Choose one player from each team to start.

4. A player from the opposing team sets the timer for 60 seconds. A player from the same team stands next to the target to track the scoring and return bottles to the flipper as needed.

5. When the opponent says "Go" and starts the timer, the player attempts to flip a bottle onto as many point squares as possible until the timer runs out. The bottle must land upright with more than half of the base touching a square to collect the points on that square.

6. When the 60 seconds is up, the player's score is recorded and play goes to the opposite team. The team that reaches 100 points first is the winner.

◎ SCORING

- ► **5 points for landing on a square with a 5**
- ► **100 points and an instant win for landing on the green 100 square**
- ► **-10 points for landing on the skull square**

 TRICK SHOT BONUS: If a player spins around 6 times before throwing their bottle, the points received for landing on a square are doubled. If the player's bottle lands on the skull, his or her team automatically loses the game.

SINGLE-PLAYER MODE

Race against the clock to land a collection of bottles on as many squares as possible within 60 seconds. Keep track of your points and play to beat your record!

NOTHIN' BUT NET

Get ready to drive your bottles to the basket in this shoot-and-score bottle-flipping showdown. Attack the rim and work the court like LeBron as you fight to earn points and establish some serious street cred. Flip a bottle onto the basket and you'll be on your way to clinching the win. Land a "swish" and you'll rack up points like a true baller.

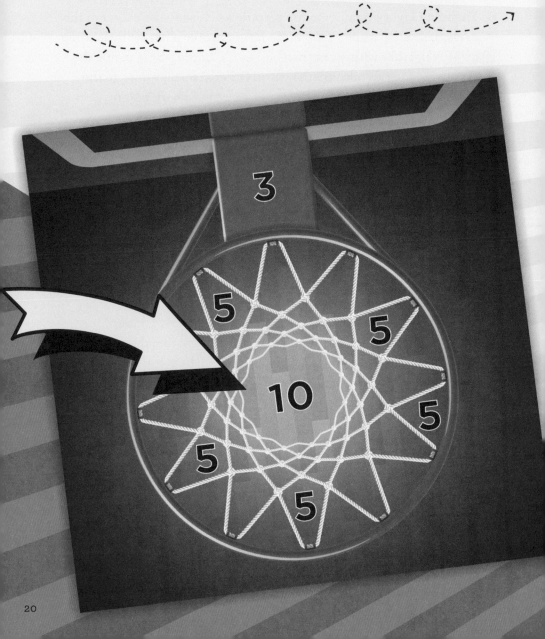

MULTIPLAYER MODE

1. Place the target on a sturdy table or floor.

2. Decide how far away a player should stand from the target and mark this distance with an object or a piece of tape.

3. Choose one player from each team to start.

4. The first player attempts to flip a bottle as close to the center of the basketball hoop as possible. If the player scores a basket by landing a bottle upright with more than half of the bottle's base inside the rim, he or she can take another turn. Otherwise, play goes to the opposing team. The bottle must land upright to earn points.

5. The first team to earn 50 points wins.

◎ SCORING

▶ **10 points for a "swish" when the bottle lands in the center of the net.**

▶ **5 points for a flip that lands touching only the net**

▶ **3 points for a flip that lands touching any part of the rim**

 TRICK SHOT BONUS: If a player shoots from under his or her leg and the bottle lands inside the rim, the points earned are doubled. If the player "swishes" the bottle using this trick shot, his or her team automatically wins the game.

SINGLE-PLAYER MODE

Practice your hoop skills and count how many baskets you can get in a row. For an added challenge, record how long it takes you to reach 50 points.

FULL COUNT FLIP

Pitch a perfect game with Full Count Flip. Without a batter in sight, it's just you, the bottle, and the mitt vying for strikeout glory. You'll be throwing fouls if your pitches are off the glove, so use this game to hone your pitching accuracy. Flip it old school or try for a trick pitch through the legs, and secure your spot as a Hall of Famer.

Extra item needed:
cell phone or kitchen timer

MULTIPLAYER MODE

1. Place the target on a sturdy table or floor.

2. Decide how far away a player should stand from the target and mark this distance with an object or a piece of tape.

3. Choose one player from each team to start.

4. The player, or "pitcher," attempts to flip a bottle onto one of the catcher's mitts for a "strike." A flip that is not a strike is considered a "ball." More than half of the bottle's base must be on the mitt in order for the strike to count. The bottle must also remain standing after the toss in order for it to count.

5. The player flips bottles until he or she lands three strikes or four balls.

6. The first team to earn 100 points wins the game.

◎ SCORING

▶ Each strikeout earns a team 10 points.

▶ Each turn that doesn't result in a strikeout is considered a "walk" and earns 0 points.

 TRICK SHOT: If a pitcher throws a strike from between his or her legs while facing away from the target, that player's team earns three strikeouts (30 points).

SINGLE-PLAYER MODE

The best pitchers practice often! Follow the Multiplayer Mode rules and see how many pitches, or flips, you need to earn a strikeout or to earn 100 points.

FLIPPIN' BURGERS

Fast food just got even faster with this delicious, grade A target game. It's time to beef up your skills as you try to outdo your competitor by serving up some stellar flips and landing them on the burgers with the highest point value. Are you hungry for a win? Work those patties like a boss!

Extra item needed:
cell phone or kitchen timer

MULTIPLAYER MODE

1. Place the target on a sturdy table or floor.

2. Decide how far away a player should stand from the target and mark this distance with an object or a piece of tape. Arrange 6–12 water bottles in a line next to the marker.

3. Choose one player from each team to start.

4. A player from the opposing team sets the timer for 60 seconds. A player from the same team stands next to the target to track the scoring and return bottles to the flipper as needed.

5. When the opponent says "Go" and starts the timer, the player has 60 seconds to "serve up" as many burgers as possible by flipping a bottle onto a burger target. When a bottle lands upright and more than half of the bottle's base is touching the burger, the player's team earns points.

6. When the 60 seconds are up, the player's score is recorded and play goes to the opposite team. The team that reaches 100 points first is the winner.

◎ SCORING

▶ Earn 20 points for flipping a bottle onto a burger marked 20.

▶ Earn 10 points for flipping a bottle onto a burger marked 10.

▶ Earn 5 points for flipping a bottle onto a burger marked 5.

▶ Earn 0 points for fries.

 TRICK SHOT: A player who flips a bottle off the top of his or her foot onto a burger marked 5 or 10 earns double the points. If the bottle lands on the burger marked 20, the player's team automatically wins.

SINGLE-PLAYER MODE

Order up! How many burgers can you "flip" in 60 seconds? Practice your trick shot to earn double the points and beat your record!

FLIP OR FLOP

Flip-flop, you don't stop. This no-frills game is all about accuracy. Flip your way to the winner's circle by landing on a 10, or flop your way to a swift loss by landing on the goose eggs. Once you've perfected your flip, test out your trick shots and keep the beach party going.

 Extra item needed:
cell phone or kitchen timer

0   10   0

10   0   10

10   0   10

MULTIPLAYER MODE

1. Place the target on a sturdy table or floor.

2. Decide how far away a player should stand from the target and mark this distance with an object or a piece of tape.

3. Choose one player from each team to start.

4. The first player attempts to flip a bottle and land it on a "flip," a pair of sandals marked with a 10. More than half of the bottle must be on a sandal in order to earn points. The bottle must also remain standing after the toss.

5. If the bottle lands on a sandal of any kind, the score is recorded and the player's turn continues. If it lands outside of a sandal, the player's turn ends and play reverts to the other team. If the bottle lands on the purple pair of sandals at the center of the target, the player must do the trick shot for each remaining turn!

6. The first team to earn 100 points wins the game.

◎ SCORING

▶ 10 points for flipping a bottle onto a "flip" (a pair of sandals marked "10")

▶ 0 points for flipping a bottle onto a "flop" (a pair of sandals marked with a "0")

 TRICK SHOT: A player who lands their bottle on a flip while continuously hopping on one foot earns his or her team 30 points!

SINGLE-PLAYER MODE

Use the same rules from Multiplayer Mode, but if you land on a flop while in Single-Player Mode, you lose 10 points.

BOTTLE ON THE BULLSEYE

If you mess with the bull, you'll get the horns. Turn this classic bullseye dart game into a fliptastic bottle championship. Aim for the center for maximum points or try some cowboy-style stunts like flipping two bottles at a time to take your opponent down like a pro. Stay on target with your flip game and you could go down in bullseye history.

1

3

5

10

20

MULTIPLAYER MODE

1. Place the target on a sturdy table or floor.

2. Decide how far away a player should stand from the target and mark this distance with an object or a piece of tape.

3. Choose one player from each team to start.

4. The player attempts to flip a bottle and land it as close to the center of the target as possible. It must land upright with more than half of the bottle's base touching a ring to earn points. The turns alternate between teams, with each player getting three flips per turn.

5. The first team to earn 50 points wins the game.

◎ SCORING

▶ Earn 20 points for flipping a bottle onto the yellow bullseye rings.

▶ Earn 10 points for flipping a bottle onto the red target rings.

▶ Earn 5 points for flipping a bottle onto the blue target rings.

▶ Earn 3 points for flipping a bottle onto the black target rings.

▶ Earn 1 point for flipping a bottle onto the white target rings.

TRICK SHOT: If a player flips two bottles at once and lands both inside the target, he or she can add both ring values to their score. If one lands outside of the target, the turn ends and play goes to the other team. If both bottles land touching the bullseye, the player's team automatically wins the game!

SINGLE-PLAYER MODE

Practice your techniques in one of the oldest party games out there. How many times can you land a bullseye? Use the Multiplayer Mode rules and see how many flips it takes you to earn those 50 points.

FLIPPIN' BOXCARS

Take your chances with this high-rolling target challenge. With two chances to score points by landing your lucky bottles on a winning pair of dice, you'll need to work the table like it's Vegas. Every flip is a dangerous gamble: score two 6s in a row and you're an instant boxcar champion, but land on two 1s and the curse of the snake eyes is upon you.

 TRICK SHOT: An over-the-shoulder toss performed with the player's back toward the target doubles the number of points received during the player's turn.

MULTIPLAYER MODE

1. Place the target on a sturdy table or floor.

2. Decide how far away a player should stand from the target and mark this distance with an object or a piece of tape.

3. Choose one player from each team to start.

4. The player attempts to flip (or "roll") a bottle onto a die with the highest value. Each player will have two flips ("rolls") per turn.

5. When a player rolls their bottle and lands on a die, he or she earns the number of points shown on the die. If the second roll also lands on a die, the player adds up their points and play reverts to the other team. Landing two 6s in a row (a "boxcar") wins the game, while landing two 1s in a row ("snake eyes") loses the game. In order to earn points, the bottle must land upright with more than half of the base on a target.

6. The first team to earn 50 points wins the game.

◎ SCORING

▶ 6 points for each bottle that lands on a die with 6 dots

▶ 5 points for each bottle that lands on a die with 5 dots

▶ 4 points for each bottle that lands on a die with 4 dots

▶ 3 points for each bottle that lands on a die with 3 dots

▶ 2 points for each bottle that lands on a die with 2 dots

▶ 1 point for each bottle that lands on a die with 1 dot

▶ 14 points when a player lands on two dice that add up to 7

▶ 0 points for a bottle that flips outside of a dice target

SINGLE-PLAYER MODE

Use the Multiplayer Mode rules, but keep track of your score and try to beat your personal best!

GLAZE OF GLORY

If you have an appetite for glory, you're more than ready to enter this doughnut competition and win your way to pastry perfection. Not all of these doughnuts are tasty and sweet—hit the poisonous pink and your sugar high will come crashing down. Sprinkle your game with some extra tricks, and you'll be rewarded with the sweet taste of victory.

MULTIPLAYER MODE

1. Place the target on a sturdy table or floor.

2. Decide how far away a player should stand from the target and mark this distance with an object or a piece of tape.

3. Choose one player from each team to start.

4. The player attempts to flip a bottle onto a doughnut. If their bottle lands on a doughnut, with more than half of the bottle's base touching the doughnut, they get another flip. If the bottle doesn't land on a doughnut, the turn is over and play reverts to the other team.

5. The first team to earn 12 points wins the game.

◎ SCORING

- ▶ 1 point for landing a flip on a doughnut
- ▶ 2 points for landing on "double dip," the upper-left corner doughnut
- ▶ -2 points for landing on "poisonous pink," the center doughnut

 TRICK SHOT: If a player flips a bottle while lying on the ground (with his or her head pointed toward the target), that player's team earns 6 doughnuts. If it lands on poisonous pink, the player's team automatically loses the game.

SINGLE-PLAYER MODE

Use Multiplayer Mode rules and keep track of your points to beat your personal best.

THE SLAP SHOT FLIP

Win the Stanley Cup of bottle flipping with this bottle-flipping faceoff. Aim for the goal to edge out the competition, and avoid the goalie's mitt if you know what's good for you. Hit your opponents where it hurts and try the 20-point trick shot. With enough ice-cold precision, you'll be making a fast break toward victory.

MULTIPLAYER MODE

1. Place the target on a sturdy table or floor.

2. Decide how far away a player should stand from the target and mark this distance with an object or a piece of tape.

3. Choose one player from each team to start.

4. The player attempts to flip the bottle, or "puck," onto the goal and earn as many points as possible. If the bottle lands in the goal, with more than half of the bottle's base touching the goal, the player gets another flip of the puck. If the bottle doesn't land on the goal, the turn is over and play reverts to the other team.

5. The first team to reach 50 points wins.

◎ SCORING

▶ **20 points for landing a flip between the goalie's legs**

▶ **10 points for landing a flip on a corner of the goal**

▶ **3 points for landing a flip anywhere on the goalie, including his stick**

▶ **0 points for landing a flip outside of the goal**

▶ **-10 points for landing a flip on the goalie's mitt, marked with a skull**

 TRICK SHOT: If the player throws while blindfolded and the bottle lands on the target, the number of points awarded automatically doubles. If the "puck" lands on the 20-point mark, the player's team automatically wins the game.

SINGLE-PLAYER MODE

Take on the goalie to test your skills using the Multiplayer Mode rules. How many flips does it take you to earn 50 points?

THE BOTTLE ROCKET

Flip your bottle out of this world with the Bottle Rocket. Keeping your bottle in orbit is no easy maneuver, but the atmosphere is perfect for a galactic win. Blast that bottle onto any of the planets, but keep in mind that a solar landing will burn up your score.

MULTIPLAYER MODE

1. Place the target on a sturdy table or floor.

2. Decide how far away a player should stand from the target and mark this distance with an object or a piece of tape.

3. Choose one player from each team to start.

4. The player attempts to flip the bottle onto a planet or star (other than the sun) to earn points. If the bottle lands with more than half of the bottle's base touching a planet or star, the player gets another turn. If the bottle lands on the sun, the team automatically loses the game.

5. If the bottle doesn't land on a planet or star, the turn is over and play reverts to the other team.

6. The first team to reach 50 points wins.

◎ SCORING

▶ **5 points when you flip your bottle onto a planet or star (other than the sun)**

▶ **0 points when you flip your bottle off the target or outside of a planet or star**

TRICK SHOT: If a player releases the bottle in an upside-down position and it lands on a planet or star other than the sun, the player's team earns double the points. If the upside-down-release bottle lands on the sun, the player's team automatically wins the game!

SINGLE-PLAYER MODE

Take on this galactic adventure using the Multiplayer Mode rules. Try to beat your own record before you burn up.

BABY BOTTLE CHALLENGE

Find out who the cry babies are in this Baby Bottle Challenge. Flip your bottles to quiet this baby down, or endure the terrifying consequences if you land on the dirty diaper. Leave your opponents kicking and screaming as you flip your bottles like a pro nanny.

Extra item needed: Try using a baby bottle partially filled with milk for a fun twist!

MULTIPLAYER MODE

1. Place the target on a sturdy table or floor.

2. Decide how far away a player should stand from the target and mark this distance with an object or a piece of tape.

3. Choose one player from each team to start.

4. The player attempts to flip their bottle onto the baby, avoiding the diaper at all costs. If the bottle lands with more than half of the bottle's base touching the baby, the player gets another turn.

5. If the bottle lands on the baby's diaper or lands without touching the baby, the turn is over and play reverts to the other team.

6. The first team to earn 100 points wins.

◎ SCORING

- ▶ 20 points for landing a flip in the baby's mouth
- ▶ 10 points for landing a flip on the baby's body
- ▶ -10 points for landing a flip on the baby's diaper

 TRICK SHOT: If a player holds the bottle between his or her pinky fingers and flips it onto the target, the player's team gets double points! If the bottle lands on the diaper during a pinky flip, the player's team automatically wins the game.

SINGLE-PLAYER MODE

Show this baby who's in charge when you play solo using the Multiplayer Mode rules but trying for your own personal best.

STUNT LOG

Use this stunt log to record your most epic bottle flipping moments. Friends can brag about their coolest stunts here, too. If you want to make sure everyone believes you, have a witness sign his or her name.

Date	Name of Flipper	Trick or Stunt	Witness Signature

FLIPPIN' AWESOME SCORE CARDS

Round	Team #1 Score	Team #2 Score
1		
2		
3		
4		
5		
6		
7		
8		
9		
10		
11		
12		
13		
14		
15		
16		
17		
18		
19		
20		
TOTAL SCORE:		

FLIPPIN' AWESOME SCORE CARDS

Round	Team #1 Score	Team #2 Score
1		
2		
3		
4		
5		
6		
7		
8		
9		
10		
11		
12		
13		
14		
15		
16		
17		
18		
19		
20		
TOTAL SCORE:		

FLIPPIN' AWESOME SCORE CARDS

Round	Team #1 Score	Team #2 Score
1		
2		
3		
4		
5		
6		
7		
8		
9		
10		
11		
12		
13		
14		
15		
16		
17		
18		
19		
20		
TOTAL SCORE:		

FLIPPIN' AWESOME SCORE CARDS

Round	Team #1 Score	Team #2 Score
1		
2		
3		
4		
5		
6		
7		
8		
9		
10		
11		
12		
13		
14		
15		
16		
17		
18		
19		
20		
TOTAL SCORE:		

FLIPPIN' AWESOME SCORE CARDS

Round	Team #1 Score	Team #2 Score
1		
2		
3		
4		
5		
6		
7		
8		
9		
10		
11		
12		
13		
14		
15		
16		
17		
18		
19		
20		
TOTAL SCORE:		

FLIPPIN' AWESOME SCORE CARDS

Round	Team #1 Score	Team #2 Score
1		
2		
3		
4		
5		
6		
7		
8		
9		
10		
11		
12		
13		
14		
15		
16		
17		
18		
19		
20		
TOTAL SCORE:		

FLIPPIN' AWESOME SCORE CARDS

Round	Team #1 Score	Team #2 Score
1		
2		
3		
4		
5		
6		
7		
8		
9		
10		
11		
12		
13		
14		
15		
16		
17		
18		
19		
20		
TOTAL SCORE:		

FLIPPIN' AWESOME SCORE CARDS

Round	Team #1 Score	Team #2 Score
1		
2		
3		
4		
5		
6		
7		
8		
9		
10		
11		
12		
13		
14		
15		
16		
17		
18		
19		
20		
TOTAL SCORE:		

FLIPPIN' AWESOME SCORE CARDS

Round	Team #1 Score	Team #2 Score
1		
2		
3		
4		
5		
6		
7		
8		
9		
10		
11		
12		
13		
14		
15		
16		
17		
18		
19		
20		
TOTAL SCORE:		

FLIPPIN' AWESOME SCORE CARDS

Round	Team #1 Score	Team #2 Score
1		
2		
3		
4		
5		
6		
7		
8		
9		
10		
11		
12		
13		
14		
15		
16		
17		
18		
19		
20		
TOTAL SCORE:		

FLIPPIN' AWESOME SCORE CARDS

Round	Team #1 Score	Team #2 Score
1		
2		
3		
4		
5		
6		
7		
8		
9		
10		
11		
12		
13		
14		
15		
16		
17		
18		
19		
20		
TOTAL SCORE:		

FLIPPIN' AWESOME SCORE CARDS

Round	Team #1 Score	Team #2 Score
1		
2		
3		
4		
5		
6		
7		
8		
9		
10		
11		
12		
13		
14		
15		
16		
17		
18		
19		
20		
TOTAL SCORE:		

FLIPPIN' AWESOME SCORE CARDS

Round	Team #1 Score	Team #2 Score
1		
2		
3		
4		
5		
6		
7		
8		
9		
10		
11		
12		
13		
14		
15		
16		
17		
18		
19		
20		
TOTAL SCORE:		

FLIPPIN' AWESOME SCORE CARDS

Round	Team #1 Score	Team #2 Score
1		
2		
3		
4		
5		
6		
7		
8		
9		
10		
11		
12		
13		
14		
15		
16		
17		
18		
19		
20		
TOTAL SCORE:		

FLIPPIN' AWESOME SCORE CARDS

Round	Team #1 Score	Team #2 Score
1		
2		
3		
4		
5		
6		
7		
8		
9		
10		
11		
12		
13		
14		
15		
16		
17		
18		
19		
20		
TOTAL SCORE:		

FLIPPIN' AWESOME SCORE CARDS

Round	Team #1 Score	Team #2 Score
1		
2		
3		
4		
5		
6		
7		
8		
9		
10		
11		
12		
13		
14		
15		
16		
17		
18		
19		
20		
TOTAL SCORE:		

FLIPPIN' AWESOME SCORE CARDS

Round	Team #1 Score	Team #2 Score
1		
2		
3		
4		
5		
6		
7		
8		
9		
10		
11		
12		
13		
14		
15		
16		
17		
18		
19		
20		
TOTAL SCORE:		

FLIPPIN' AWESOME SCORE CARDS

Round	Team #1 Score	Team #2 Score
1		
2		
3		
4		
5		
6		
7		
8		
9		
10		
11		
12		
13		
14		
15		
16		
17		
18		
19		
20		
TOTAL SCORE:		

FLIPPIN' AWESOME SCORE CARDS

Round	Team #1 Score	Team #2 Score
1		
2		
3		
4		
5		
6		
7		
8		
9		
10		
11		
12		
13		
14		
15		
16		
17		
18		
19		
20		
TOTAL SCORE:		

FLIPPIN' AWESOME SCORE CARDS

Round	Team #1 Score	Team #2 Score
1		
2		
3		
4		
5		
6		
7		
8		
9		
10		
11		
12		
13		
14		
15		
16		
17		
18		
19		
20		
TOTAL SCORE:		

FLIPPIN' AWESOME SCORE CARDS

Round	Team #1 Score	Team #2 Score
1		
2		
3		
4		
5		
6		
7		
8		
9		
10		
11		
12		
13		
14		
15		
16		
17		
18		
19		
20		
TOTAL SCORE:		

FLIPPIN' AWESOME SCORE CARDS

Round	Team #1 Score	Team #2 Score
1		
2		
3		
4		
5		
6		
7		
8		
9		
10		
11		
12		
13		
14		
15		
16		
17		
18		
19		
20		
TOTAL SCORE:		

FLIPPIN' AWESOME SCORE CARDS

Round	Team #1 Score	Team #2 Score
1		
2		
3		
4		
5		
6		
7		
8		
9		
10		
11		
12		
13		
14		
15		
16		
17		
18		
19		
20		
TOTAL SCORE:		

FLIPPIN' AWESOME SCORE CARDS

Round	Team #1 Score	Team #2 Score
1		
2		
3		
4		
5		
6		
7		
8		
9		
10		
11		
12		
13		
14		
15		
16		
17		
18		
19		
20		
TOTAL SCORE:		